Islam

Sue Penney

Heinemann
LIBRARY

H www.heinemann.co.uk
Visit our website to find out more information about Heinemann Library books.

To order:
☎ Phone 44 (0) 1865 888066
▤ Send a fax to 44 (0) 1865 314091
▢ Visit the Heinemann Bookshop at www.heinemann.co.uk to browse our catalogue and order online.

First published in Great Britain by Heinemann Library, Halley Court, Jordan Hill, Oxford OX2 8EJ
a division of Reed Educational and Professional Publishing Ltd.
Heinemann is a registered trademark of Reed Educational & Professional Publishing Ltd.

OXFORD MELBOURNE AUCKLAND JOHANNESBURG BLANTYRE
GABORONE IBADAN PORTSMOUTH (NH) USA CHICAGO

Designed by Ken Vail Graphic Design
Originated by Universal
Printed by Wing King Tong in Hong Kong

ISBN 0 431 09313 X (hardback)   ISBN 0 431 09320 2 (paperback)
05 04 03 02 01   05 04 03 02 01
10 9 8 7 6 5 4 3 2   10 9 8 7 6 5 4 3 2

British Library Cataloguing in Publication Data

Penney, Sue
Judaism. – (World Beliefs and Cultures)
1. Islam – Juvenile literature
1. Title
297

Acknowledgements
The Publishers would like to thank the following for permission to reproduce copyright material:
Roman transliteration of the Holy Qu'ran with English translation, Abdullah Yusuf Ali, Sh Muhammad Ashraf Publishers, Pakistan.

The Publishers would like to thank the following for permission to reproduce photographs: Ancient Art and Architecture p.35; Carlos Reyes-Manzo/Andes Press Agency, p.40; Circa Photo Library/William Hotlby, pp.25, 31, 32, 41; Photoedit, p.18, Stock Boston, p.42. All other photos: Peter SandersCover photograph reproduced with permission of Peter Sanders.

Our thanks to Philip Emmett for his comments in the preparation of this book.

Every effort has been made to contact copyright holders of any material reproduced in this book. Any omissions will be rectified in subsequent printings if notice is given to the Publisher.

Words appearing in the text in bold, **like this**, are explained in the Glossary.

Contents

Dates: in this book, dates are followed by the letters BCE (Before Common Era) or CE (Common Era). This is instead of using BC (Before Christ) and AD (*Anno Domini*, meaning in the year of our Lord). The date numbers are the same in both systems.

Introducing Islam

Islam is the religion of people called Muslims. The word Islam and the word Muslim both come from an **Arabic** word which is best translated as 'submission'. Submission means 'to place under' – in other words, to accept that someone else is more important than yourself, and to obey them. Muslims believe that they submit to God, whom they call **Allah**. This submission is not like being a slave, obeying without question and with no involvement. It is an active decision to live their lives as Allah wants.

▲ *Muslims are part of many different cultures.*

What do Muslims believe?

Muslims believe that there is one God, Allah. They believe that Allah is **eternal**, in other words, he was never born and he will never die. He has always been there. He is all-powerful and knows everything. He created the universe, the world and everything in it. He cares about what he made. He created human beings, and they have a duty to worship him, in return for all that he has done for them.

Muslims believe that the entire universe is Muslim, because it follows the laws that Allah laid down. However, Allah gave human beings free will – the freedom to choose right or wrong. This means that they are able to choose to be Muslim. Believing in Allah is not enough – they must live in the right way too. Muslims call this **niyyah** – intention. They believe that the intention to live a good life is vital to being a Muslim. This does not mean that they expect everyone to succeed all the time, but it is necessary to try as hard as they can. They believe that Allah is merciful and will judge what their intentions were.

Prophets

Muslims believe that human beings can only know about Allah because he has sent **prophets** to Earth. A prophet is a messenger from God who tells people how God wants them to live. Muslims believe that there have been 124,000 prophets, over thousands of years, and all of them were Muslims. The first prophet was Adam, the first man. The last and the most important prophet was a man called Muhammad. He was born in the country we now call Saudi Arabia in the year 570 CE. Muslims believe that Muhammad received messages from Allah, given to him by an angel. These messages were the words of Allah and can never be changed. They were collected together to form the Muslims' holy book, which is called the **Qur'an**.

The Shahadah

The most important beliefs of Islam are summed up in the **Shahadah**. This is also called the Declaration of Faith. In Arabic it is 'La ilaha illa-Llah, Muhamadur rasulu-Allah'. This is usually translated as 'There is no God except Allah, and Muhammad is the messenger of Allah.' These are the first words said to a new-born Muslim baby, and the last words said by a Muslim who is dying, if they are still able to speak. If the person cannot speak, the words are said by other people present. They are the first words that a Muslim says on waking up, and the last words said before they go to sleep. The Shahadah also forms part of the Call to Prayer (see page 23).

▶ *The Shahadah made into a picture.*

Islam fact check

- Muslims believe that there is only one God, whom they call Allah.

- The Muslim place of worship is called a **mosque**.

- The Muslim holy book is called the Qur'an.

- The Muslim calendar dates from 622 CE.
  This is when Muhammad moved to Madinah, an event called the **hijrah**.

- The symbol most often used for Islam is a crescent moon and a star. No one really knows where this symbol came from, but many people believe it comes from the fact that Islam has its roots in desert countries. People travelled at night when it was cooler, and used the moon and stars to guide them, just as their religion guides them through life.

- There are over 1.2 billion Muslims in the world today, living in almost every country in the world.

- About 3 million Muslims live in the USA, about 1.5 million live in Britain, and about 220,000 live in Australia.

- In most of the countries in northern Africa and the Middle East, over half the population are Muslim.

- In Europe, Islam is the second largest religion after Christianity.

The life of Muhammad

Muhammad was born in the city of Makkah, in the country we now call Saudi Arabia. Muslims believe he was born in the year 570 CE, on the twelfth day of the third month. His mother, Amina, was a widow, because Muhammad's father had died before he was born. When Muhammad was six, his mother died and he was cared for by his grandfather. Two years later his grandfather died, and Muhammad's uncle began to look after him.

▲ These traders today still live and work in similar ways to Muhammad.

You can find the places mentioned in this book on the map on page 44.

Makkah was an important trading centre, and Muhammad's uncle was a trader. From about the age of twelve, Muhammad began helping his uncle. By the time he was adult, Muhammad had become well known for his honesty and goodness. He was given the nickname Al-Amin, which means 'the trustworthy one'. He began working for a wealthy woman called Khadijah, who was also a trader. When Muhammad was 25, he and Khadijah were married. Muhammad was respected, he was rich, he was happily married. It seemed that his life had everything he could possibly want.

However, Muhammad had always been a thoughtful man, and there were evidently times when he needed to be by himself. He needed to **meditate** about his life and the things that were happening in the world around him. He was unhappy about what he saw in the life of Makkah. There were wealthy people, but many of them spent their days in gambling, drinking and fighting. The rich cheated the poor. The worship of **idols** was common, and often included **sacrifices**. Muhammad was sure that these things were wrong.

One night, when he was about 40 years old, Muhammad was meditating in a cave on Mount Hira. Muslims believe that he saw the angel Jibril (sometimes spelled Gabriel). Jibril was a messenger from **Allah**, giving Muhammad words of revelation that he must read. Muslims believe that this was the first of the **revelations** of the **Qur'an**. As Muhammad stood up and walked out of the cave, he heard the angel say, 'Muhammad! You are Allah's messenger!'

Muhammad was terrified by this experience. He feared that he might be going mad, or that an evil force was trying to make him claim special powers for himself. He returned home and told Khadijah what had happened. She comforted him and went to talk to her cousin, an old man who was a devout Christian, and whose judgement she respected. He was sure that Muhammad had indeed seen a messenger from God. Khadijah became the first person to believe in the words that Muhammad spoke.

Some months later, Muhammad had another revelation. Then there was a gap of two years before the revelations began again. After this, Muhammad continued to receive messages and instructions from Allah for the rest of his life. For several years, Muhammad did not speak of his experiences except to his friends and family. Then the angel told him that he must go out and preach to the people of Makkah. His message was not well received. The people did not like being told that the way they lived was wrong. They made a lot of money from people coming to worship the idols, and they did not want to get rid of them in order to worship only Allah.

▲ *The Great Mosque in Makkah today, with Mount Hira in the background.*

After several years, men from the neighbouring town of Yathrib heard Muhammad preaching. They were impressed and asked him to go to their town and become a religious leader there. At last Muhammad agreed. His journey to Yathrib (later called Madinah) is called the **hijrah**.

The Hadith

The most important teachings of Islam are those of the Qur'an, which Muslims believe were Allah's words, given to Muhammad by the angel Jibril. They also have enormous respect for the **Hadith**, which means 'traditions'. The Hadith are traditional teachings which go back to the time of Muhammad. There are two sorts of Hadith: the sacred and the prophetic. The sacred Hadith are so called because Muslims believe that they are teachings that came from Allah, although they were not part of the revelations of the Qur'an. The prophetic Hadith are teachings that were given by Muhammad himself, based on experiences in his life. They are valued very highly because Muslims respect Muhammad so much. Muslims today who are faced with a problem or difficulty and cannot find an answer in the Qur'an will look in the Hadith for guidance. This tells them what Muhammad said or did in the same or a similar situation.

The hijrah

▲ The Mosque of the Prophet in Madinah today.

Muhammad made the dangerous journey to Yathrib (Madinah) in 622 CE. Yathrib was about 320 km from Makkah. The journey was dangerous because some of the people in Makkah had been very unhappy at what Muhammad was teaching. They wanted to get rid of him, and in the desert it would be easy to ambush and kill him. There are several stories in the Muslim tradition about how **Allah** protected Muhammad on the journey. For example, they say that he was hiding in a cave when his enemies came right to the entrance, but because a spider had built its web and a bird was nesting there, they did not search it.

You can find the places mentioned in this book on the map on page 44.

When Muhammad arrived in Yathrib, he was treated as an honoured **prophet**, a messenger from God. Everyone wanted him to go and stay in their house. To avoid offending anyone, Muhammad said he would let his camel choose where he was going to live. The camel knelt down at a spot where dates were laid out to dry. Muhammad bought the land and built a house there. Later, in part of the same site, he built a place of worship, where Muslims could meet for prayer. The site is still preserved and respected by Muslims as being the first **mosque** in the world.

Muhammad became a religious leader and also the leader of the city. Many people listened to his preaching, and began to follow the new religion. It became so popular that the city became known as Madinat-al-nabi, which means 'the City of the Prophet'. Later, this name was shortened to Madinah, which is the name still used today. The journey to Madinah was called the **hijrah**, which means 'the migration'. Muslims recognized that this was a very important event, so they began to number the years after it. The years of the Muslim calendar are therefore followed by the letters AH – After the Hijrah.

War with Makkah

Muhammad worked in Madinah for ten years, teaching and preaching. The new religion grew and developed, as Muhammad shared the instructions that he was receiving from Allah. The people of Makkah were not happy at the fact that it was becoming stronger and stronger. They began to cause trouble for Muhammad and his followers. There were many small fights between the two sides, and there were two major battles. The first of these was at Badr in 624 CE, and was won by the Muslims. The second was at Uhud in 625 CE, when neither side could claim victory.

Muhammad still wanted to return to Makkah, and in 628 CE he received a message from Allah which told him that he would soon return to Makkah in triumph. He went to Makkah with a group of his followers, and the Makkans made a treaty with him which allowed Muslims to travel to Makkah safely. Muhammad returned to Madinah. Two years later, the Makkans broke the treaty, and Muhammad set out with an army of 10,000 men.

The people of Makkah surrendered without a fight, and Muhammad claimed the city for Islam. Before long, everyone in Makkah accepted the new religion. The **idols** were thrown out of the city and it became a holy city dedicated to Allah. No one who was not a Muslim was allowed to go there. This rule still applies today.

Muhammad returned to Madinah and spent the next two years preaching. He died of a fever on 12 Rabi-ul-Awwal 11 AH (7 June 632 CE). He was buried where he had died, at the home of his youngest wife Aisha. The Mosque of the Prophet is built over his tomb.

'Peace be upon him'

Muslims do not regard Muhammad as being the founder of Islam. They believe that their religion was founded by Allah at the creation, and that Muhammad was the last of the prophets whom Allah sent to Earth. They respect Muhammad enormously, but they do not worship him. They believe that only Allah should be worshipped. To show their respect, whenever they mention the names of the prophets and of some of the great Muslim leaders, Muslims say the words 'Alaihi salaam' which mean 'Peace be upon him'. Whenever they mention the name of Muhammad, Muslims say 'Salla-Allah alaihi wa sallam' which means 'Peace and blessings of Allah upon him'. When writing in English, Muslims often use 'pbuh' or 'saw' (from the first letters of the **Arabic** words) to shorten the phrases. In Arabic, the language of Islam, these two phrases are written down in a special way, like this:

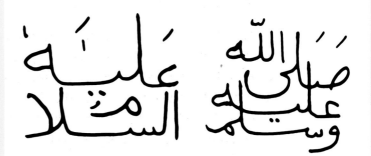

'Peace be upon him.'   'Peace and blessings of Allah upon him.'

The early history of Islam

The first khalifahs

Muhammad died in 632 CE, and his followers had to decide who was to be their new leader. Muhammad and his first wife Khadijah had had two sons, but both died in infancy. Many Muslims felt that Muhammad's son-in-law, Ali, should take over the leadership. Other Muslims wanted to hold elections and nominate Abu Bakr as leader. Abu Bakr had been one of Muhammad's closest friends, and he was the father of Muhammad's wife Aisha. Abu Bakr's supporters won, and Abu Bakr became the new leader.

The leaders were called **khalifahs**, which means 'successors'. Abu Bakr was khalifah for two years. During this time, the whole of Arabia became Muslim, and the religion was spreading into the countries round about. He chose Umar, another friend of Muhammad's, to be the next khalifah after him. Umar was khalifah for ten years, and in that time Muslim armies conquered Syria and Palestine, and began to spread into Egypt and Iran. Umar also ordered that the whole of the message that the angel Jibril had given Muhammad should be written down, while there were still people alive who remembered exactly what the words had been.

In 644 CE, Umar was murdered by one of his servants. Umar was succeeded as khalifah by Uthman, who ruled until 656 CE, when he too was murdered. The fourth khalifah was Ali, Muhammad's son-in-law who some Muslims had wanted to be the first khalifah, 24 years earlier. He ruled for five years, during which there were two rebellions against him. When he too was murdered, the position of khalifah passed to his main rival, Mu'awiya. This led to differences of opinion between Muslims about who was really a khalifah, and who the next one should be (see pages 12–13).

By 732 CE Islam had spread far beyond Arabia. The modern place names have been used on this map.

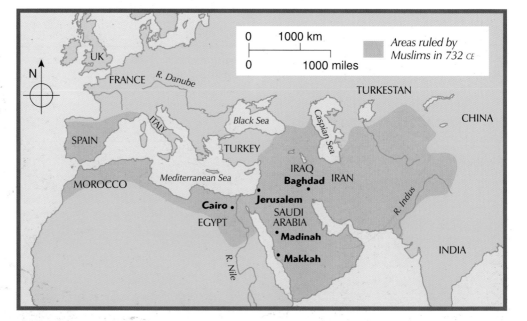

The spread of Islam

During the time of the first khalifahs, Islam spread very quickly. By the time of Muhammad's death, almost the whole of Arabia had become Muslim, and within a hundred years after his death, countries as far as Spain and India were ruled by Muslims.

In 637 CE, a Muslim army captured Jerusalem, and by 642 CE, Muslims were in control of present-day Egypt. By 700 CE, Muslims controlled almost all of the North African coast.

Jihad

Jihad means 'striving' – in other words, trying to live and do everything for the love of **Allah**. For most Muslims, this means prayer or giving extra money to charity – anything where a person makes an effort to serve Allah to the best of their ability. This is 'major jihad'. Sometimes the word jihad is used to apply to a war situation, and is translated as 'holy war'. This is 'minor jihad'. Holy wars can only be fought in defence, never as the aggressor, and there are strict rules about the way in which the war must be fought.

Where the army led, traders soon followed, and this was another way in which Islam spread. The traders took their religion with them, and became well known for the fact that they lived good lives and were honest to deal with. Many people respected them, and some decided that they wanted to become Muslims too.

Where Muslims ruled people who belonged to other religions, those people were generally tolerated so long as they did not interfere with the Muslim way of life. The **Qur'an** teaches clearly that people cannot be forced to convert to Islam. Non-Muslims had to pay a special tax, but those who became Muslims lived tax-free.

▼ The prayer room in the Great Mosque in Cordoba, Spain, dates from the 8–10th centuries CE. The building is now used as a Christian church.

Sunni and Shi'ah Muslims

For 24 years after the death of Muhammad there were differences of opinion among Muslims about who should be the **khalifah**. Then, after the murder of Ali, Mu'awiya became the leader. He was a member of the Ummayad family, who were the most important tribe in Makkah. This caused an extra problem. Many Muslims did not want to be led by a member of the family that had been responsible for persecuting Muslims in Makkah. They claimed that the position of khalifah should stay in Muhammad's family, and now that Ali was dead the next khalifah should be his son, Hasan.

The political differences of opinion led to two branches of Islam developing. The group who supported Ali became known as the Shi'at Ali, which means 'the Party of Ali'. They are now known as Shi'ah Muslims. The other group took the name Sunni, from the word sunnah, which means 'authority'. They believe that they are the people who follow the line of authority from Muhammad. Both of the groups still follow all the teachings of Islam.

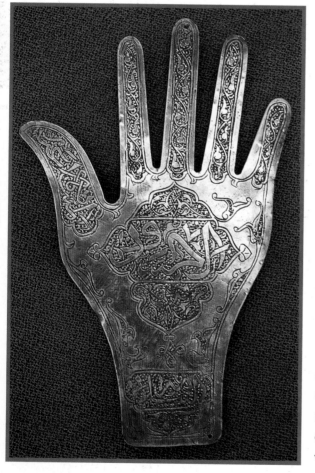

Sunni Muslims

About 90 per cent of Muslims today belong to the group called Sunnis. They believe that Muhammad intended the leader of the Muslims to be elected. This would mean that the best person could be chosen, rather than that leadership should automatically go to the son of the previous leader. They believe that the **Qur'an** and the **Hadith** show the way that Muslims should live.

Shi'ah Muslims

About ten per cent of Muslims today make up the Shi'ah group, but that number is increasing. Shi'ahs do not accept the first three khalifahs, and say that Ali was the first true khalifah. Shi'ahs are totally dedicated to their leaders, and follow them with a loyalty that other people sometimes find difficult to understand. Some Shi'ah groups are made up of people who believe that violence is justified when fighting for justice.

▲ The hand of Fatima is a symbol of Shi'ah Muslims. The thumb and fingers represent Muhammad, his daughter Fatima, her husband Ali and their sons Hasan and Husain.

This belief comes partly from their beliefs about **martyrs**. Islam teaches that a martyr – someone who dies for what they believe – will go straight to **Allah** and live in **Paradise**. In Muslim teachings, Paradise is a garden of happiness for life after death. Believing this means that some Muslims feel that giving up their life for their beliefs is a price well worth paying, because their reward will be so great.

Imams

All Muslim religious leaders are called **imams**, but the title has a special meaning for Shi'ah Muslims. Shi'ahs believe that there were twelve imams (some Shi'ahs say seven) who were given special powers by Allah, just as Muhammad was. They believe that the first imam was Ali, whose power passed to his son, and so on. The last imam, called the Mahdi, did not die, but disappeared mysteriously in 880 CE. They believe that one day he will return, and bring about the end of the world. Until he does, the teaching of the imams is in the hands of 'Doctors of the Law', called **Ayatollahs**. Ayatollah means 'mark of Allah' and so describes someone who bears the mark of Allah in the way that they behave and in their thinking. In 1979, the Ayatollah Khomeini removed the leader of Iran from power and set up a religious state. Shi'ah Islam is now the state religion in Iran.

▼ *Shi'ah Muslim men taking part in the festival of Ashura.*

The festival of Ashura

In the month of Muharram every year, Shi'ah Muslims take part in a festival at Karbala, where the body of Husain, one of Muhammad's grandsons, is buried. Husain was killed in battle in 681 CE, fighting for the position of khalifah. Shi'ah Muslims remember this as a time when evil (the victorious Yazid) triumphed over good (the defeated Husain). During the festival, people remember the dreadful deaths of Husain and his family. There are daily gatherings where emotions are stirred up until most people are weeping and they all promise to live their lives to ensure that evil cannot triumph again. There are processions and plays showing the events of the battle and the martyrdoms. Sometimes men in the processions gash themselves with knives and beat themselves with chains, as a way of remembering what Husain suffered.

How Muhammad received the Qur'an

▲ *Jebel Nur, the cave on Mount Hira where Muhammad had his first revelation.*

The first **revelation** of the **Qur'an** came when Muhammad was **meditating** in a cave on Mount Hira, just outside Makkah. Muslims believe he saw an angel who came towards him, carrying a roll of silk on which words were written in fiery letters. The angel said, 'Iqra!' which means 'Recite!' Like many people in those days, Muhammad could not read or write, and he said that he could not read the words. The angel repeated the command three times, and each time Muhammad said that he could not do so. He said afterwards that he felt a pressure building up inside him, and something gripping his chest and his throat so tightly that he felt he was going to die. Then he found that he was able to repeat the words.

> Recite!
> In the name of your Lord,
> Who created all humanity out of a single drop of blood!
> Speak these words aloud!
> Your Lord is the Most Generous One,
> He who taught the use of the Pen, taught man that which he did not know.
> (Surah 96:1–5)

The angel identified himself as Jibril, and told Muhammad that he was to be **Allah's** messenger. Some months later, Muhammad had another vision, when the angel appeared to him as a huge pair of eyes staring at him, and became an enormous figure whose feet touched the horizon. Whichever way he turned, Muhammad could still see the figure. Again, he was terrified.

For the rest of his life, Muhammad continued to receive messages from God. On a few occasions, he saw the angel again. Most times, the messages came as voices in his head. There is a tradition that sometimes he could hear the voices perfectly, at other times they appeared muffled.

Muhammad's visions

Muslim tradition says that Muhammad always knew when the visions were going to happen, so he would lie down, usually wrapped in the cloak which he used as blanket. He sometimes appeared very hot, even in cold weather, and would sweat a great deal. He often seemed to become unconscious. The visions always made him feel that he was close to death. When the visions came to an end, he would sit up, his normal self again, and repeat what he had been told. It was the duty of his friends as well as of Muhammad himself to memorize the words, so that nothing of the message was lost.

▲ *This handwritten copy of the Qur'an is over 200 years old.*

What Muslims believe about the Qur'an

Muslims believe that the Qur'an is made up of the direct words of Allah, given to human beings through the 'mouthpiece' of Muhammad. Muslims respect the teachings which Muhammad gave himself, but they are in a different class from the words of the Qur'an, which came from Allah. This is why they believe that the actual words of the Qur'an are so important. They are the final revelation of Allah's message to the world, and they can never be changed. Muslims do not believe that Muhammad was the first person to receive a revelation from Allah. However, they believe that the revelations given to other people (for example, the Torah of the Jews or the Gospels of the Christians) are no longer accurate. They have been changed by the people who wrote them down and by subsequent generations, so they can no longer be relied upon to be the word of Allah.

Translations

Arabic is the language of the Qur'an. It uses letters that are very different from the Roman letters used in English and most European languages. This means that an Arabic word needs to be transliterated (changed into another alphabet) as well as translated (giving its meaning). There are no exact equivalents to the sound of Arabic letters in the Roman alphabet. This means that the letters that give the sound nearest to the original have to be used. Opinions have changed about which letters should be used, and this is why many Arabic words have more than one spelling in the Roman alphabet. For example, Muhammad's name can be spelled Mohamed, Mohammad and Mahomet. Makkah is often spelled Mecca. The differences are not wrong, they are just alternatives. The spellings used in this book are the ones now thought to give the closest sound to the original word.

The Qur'an

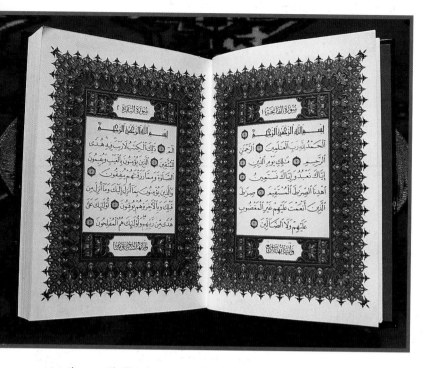

▲ *A beautifully decorated copy of the Qur'an, open at the first two surahs.*

The **Qur'an** is made up of chapters called surahs. There are 114 surahs altogether, which are of different lengths. The longest is surah 2, which has 286 verses. The shortest is surah 103, which has only three verses. Except for one (surah 9) the surahs all begin with the words 'In the name of **Allah**, the gracious, the merciful'. The surahs are not in the order that the words were received by Muhammad. Muslims believe that not long before he died, Muhammad received instructions about the order in which they were to be kept.

Muslims believe that the words of the Qur'an must be preserved exactly as they were given. Muhammad ensured that this happened by repeating all the **revelations** to his friends and family, who all learned them off by heart. In those days, not many people could read or write, and learning things like this was the usual way in which important words were remembered. The complete Qur'an was written down within twenty years of Muhammad's death, and it has never been altered.

Hafiz

Muslims believe that the Qur'an is the most important book that has ever existed, because it contains the words of Allah. To help to ensure that it can never be changed in any way, and because they believe it is so important, many Muslims learn it completely by heart. Anyone who has done this is allowed to use the title **hafiz** as part of their name. They are very respected by other Muslims.

Translations

The Qur'an has been translated into over 40 other languages, but for worship it is only ever used in **Arabic**. This is because Muslims believe that the translations can never give the exact sense of Allah's words. Even Muslims who do not speak Arabic know some of the words of the Qur'an in the original language, and use it for worship.

What does the Qur'an say?

The surahs which Muhammad received first are about the one-ness of Allah, Muhammad's role as a **prophet**, and about what will happen at the Last Judgement. Later surahs are about everyday matters such as marriage and the law, and how to live as a Muslim.

Quotes from the Qur'an

Forbidden to you for food
Are: dead meat, blood,
the flesh of swine, and that
On which has been invoked
The name other than the name of Allah.
That which has been killed by strangling
or by a violent blow,
Or by a headlong fall … (Surah 5: 4)

Those who patiently persevere,
And seek their Lord with regular prayers,
and give generously,
These overcome evil with good.
For them there is
the final attainment of the
Eternal home. (Surah 13: 22)

Allah is He, than whom
there is no other God.
He knows all things,
Both secret and open,
He, most gracious, most merciful
The sovereign, the Holy One
(Surah 59: 23)

Be steadfast in prayer
and regular in charity:
And whatever good
You send forth from your souls
You will find it with Allah:
for Allah sees all that you do.
(Surah 2: 110)

▶ *Muslims believe that learning to read the Qur'an is very important.*

How to treat the Qur'an

Muslims treat the Qur'an with enormous respect. While it is being read, they do not eat, drink or speak. They do not touch it unnecessarily, and while it is being read it is often placed on a special stool called a **kursi**. It is never allowed to touch the ground. Before beginning to read the Qur'an, Muslims wash their hands, and if they are at all dirty, they will bath completely. A woman is not permitted to touch it whilst she is menstruating. When it is not in use, it is kept on a high shelf and nothing is ever placed on top of it. It is covered to protect it from dust and damage.

Worship in the home

▲ *Reading the Qur'an at home.*

Muslims believe that their religion affects everything they do, because they have submitted their lives to **Allah**. This means that their home is the centre of their faith.

Decorations

Most Muslim families have pictures on the walls that are connected with their religion. These are always placed high up as a sign of respect. There may be pictures of important mosques, or of the **Ka'bah**, the most important **shrine** in Makkah. Pictures of people are never used, because Muhammad said they were not allowed, in case people began to worship them. Of course, most Muslims have ordinary photographs of friends and family, because these are not used as part of the religion.

The Qur'an

Reading the **Qur'an** at home together is a part of everyday life in many Muslim families. For women, who do not go to the **mosque** as often as the men, it is especially important. Children are brought up to read the Qur'an at home, and to treat it with great respect.

The five pillars of Islam

The five pillars are the foundation of Muslim worship and beliefs. They are called pillars because they support the religion in the same way that a pillar supports a building. Muslims believe that believing in and keeping the five pillars helps them to follow their religion properly.

- The first pillar is the **Shahadah**, the Declaration of Faith.

- The second pillar is **Salah**, prayer five times a day.

- The third pillar is **Zakah**, which means giving to charity.

- The fourth pillar is **Sawm**, which means **fasting**. Every year, Muslims fast during the hours of daylight for the month of Ramadan.

- The fifth pillar is **Hajj**. This is the **pilgrimage** to Makkah, which every Muslim tries to make at least once in their lifetime.

Food

Muslims believe that all food comes from God, and should be treated accordingly. Like many religions, there are restrictions about what food should and should not be eaten. For Muslims, these restrictions come from the Qur'an. Food which Muslims can eat is **halal** (permitted). Food which they cannot eat is **haram** (forbidden). Muslims are allowed to eat all fruit, grains and vegetables. They can eat fish, poultry, sheep, goats and camels, but anything that comes from a pig is strictly forbidden.

For an animal product to be halal, the animal must have been killed by the halal method. The jugular artery in the neck is severed by a razor-sharp knife. Muslims believe that this is the kindest method of killing an animal. The knife is so sharp that the animal does not feel pain, and it is unconscious before it has time to suffer. The blood drains away, so the meat does not contain any blood, which would make it haram. Whilst the knife is being used, the person using it must repeat the name of Allah. This shows that the animal is not being killed thoughtlessly, and the life is being returned to Allah who gave it. Avoiding non-halal animals does not just mean avoiding the meat. Many other foods contain animal products, so all ingredients have to be checked.

Alcohol and tobacco

Muslims are expected not to drink alcohol, because it is a drug which harms the body. They believe that since Allah made their bodies they should care for them. In Muslim countries, the possession of alcohol is against the law. Many Muslims try to avoid being anywhere where alcohol is being served or drunk. In particular, Muslims should not mention Allah or the Qur'an when they are anywhere near alcohol. For the same reasons the use of non-medical drugs is not allowed. Smoking is not forbidden but it is discouraged because of its harmful effects.

▶ *Keeping the rules about halal foods is an important part of being a Muslim.*

Worship in the mosque

Muslims believe that they can pray anywhere and at any time. Five times a day, however, they make special prayers called **Salah**. These times are between first light and sunrise, after the sun has left its highest point, between mid-afternoon and sunset, between sunset and dark, and between darkness and dawn. Muslims do not pray at dawn, noon or sunset, because they believe that this would be like pagan sun-worship.

Praying at these times involves putting everything else to one side and concentrating on **Allah**. The prayers should be performed no matter where they are or what they were doing. To do this requires preparation and discipline. Many Muslim men go to the **mosque** for prayers as often as they can. The most important prayers, which all adult males are expected to attend, are the second prayers of the day on a Friday. Women may attend the mosque, and if they do not they are expected to pray at home. Children are expected to practise Salah from about the age of seven. By the age of twelve they are expected to perform it as a religious duty.

A Muslim may pray in any clean place, and a special mat is often used. As part of the preparation, the body and clothes should be clean, and the worshipper should be dressed modestly. A man should be covered from the waist to the knees, a woman's entire body should be covered except for her face and hands. Make-up and perfume should not be worn. Like everything else in a Muslim's life, it is the **niyyah** (intention) that is most important. All the external actions of prayer are no use if the worshipper does not have the right attitude.

▼ *Wudu at a mosque in India.*

Wudu

Wudu is the special washing before prayer. This is not about being clean or dirty, it is to make the person fit to come before Allah who is holy. It also forms a break from what they were doing and gives them time to get ready to concentrate on their prayers. Some Muslims prefer to use cold water, so that they are more alert – especially for the first prayers in the morning!

Washing is always done in the same order, to make sure that nothing is forgotten. The instructions for how it should be done are in the **Qur'an**.

First, the right hand is washed, to the wrist. Then the left hand in the same way. Next, the mouth and throat, by gargling, so that the voice is clean to talk to Allah. Then the nose and face are washed, and the right arm up to the elbow, then the left. The head is wiped with a wet hand, then the ears are cleaned. Finally, the feet are washed up to the ankles, right one first. If no water is available, the person may touch clean earth or sand, and then go through the motions of washing. After washing, the person covers their head, and faces in the direction of Makkah before they begin to pray.

Rak'ahs

Salah consists of set prayers which are repeated each time. Each repetition is connected with a sequence of movements called a **rak'ah**. Two rak'ahs are made at morning prayers, four at midday and in the afternoon, three in the evening and four at night.

There are eight positions in a rak'ah. The first is when the Muslim stands to attention, showing that they intend to pray. Then they bow, stand, kneel and, in the humblest position of all, **prostrate** to touch the ground with their forehead, nose, palms of both hands, knees and toes. This position shows that they love God more than they love themselves. Then they kneel again, then prostrate again. The last movement of a rak'ah is to turn the head from side to side to greet the other people worshipping, and the two angels which Muslims believe are always with every person. At the end of a rak'ah, a Muslim may finish praying, or add private prayers of their own, which are called **du'a**.

These are the first words of the Qur'an, said by Muslims while they are in the second prayer position.

All praise be to Allah, the Lord of the Universe,
the most merciful, the most kind,
*Master of the **Day of Judgement**.*
You alone do we worship,
From you alone do we seek help.
Show us the next step along the straight path of those earning your favour.
Keep us from the path of those earning your anger, those who are going astray.

(Surah 1)

▼ *The last position of a rak'ah.*

The mosque

▲ *An open-air mosque in Jerusalem.*

Muslims believe that they can worship **Allah** in any clean place, but like many religions they prefer to have a special building where they can meet for worship. This building is called a **mosque**, or **masjid** (the **Arabic** name). Masjid means 'a place where people **prostrate** themselves' – in other words, where they bow down to worship.

There are thousands of mosques all over the world, because a Muslim community will try to build a mosque as soon as it can. Islamic law requires a mosque as soon as there are 40 adult male Muslims in any one place. Some mosques are enormous, specially built to accommodate thousands of worshippers. Others may be tiny. Some are in buildings originally built for other purposes, but used by Muslims for worship. A mosque does not have to be a building – any place used for the worship of Allah becomes a mosque, so in hot countries a mosque may be outdoors. A piece of sand marked with the direction of Makkah, and perhaps with a mat on the floor, is just as much a mosque as a fine building. In many Muslim countries, railway stations have an arrow on the wall, so that travellers know at once which direction to face for prayers. Many Muslims set aside a room or part of a room which they always use for prayer when they are at home.

Other uses for a mosque

Mosques are not only used as a place for prayer. They are used as schools, where children and adults can learn Arabic and study the **Qur'an**. From the age of four, children attend the **madrasah** to learn Arabic and be taught the Qur'an. Part of the mosque may function as a law court, where matters of Islamic law can be decided. Rooms at the mosque may be used for celebrations connected with the religion – for example, birth, marriage or funeral gatherings. They are used as community centres, where people can meet and discuss matters that affect them in their everyday lives. This is particularly important where Muslims are living in a country where most other people do not share their faith.

An essential part of all mosques is a water supply. In olden days, this was usually a fountain or just a tap in a courtyard outside the mosque. In many older mosques, this is still the case. Modern mosques usually have washrooms with rows of taps. It is where Muslims perform **wudu**, the washing before prayer. Men and women perform this washing separately. There is usually a separate room for women to pray, too. If the mosque is not big enough for this, women pray away from the men. This is to ensure that both groups can concentrate on Allah.

Where a mosque has been specially built, it usually has a dome and at least one tall tower called a **minaret**. The dome helps to create a feeling of space inside the mosque, and helps the voice of the **imam** to be heard when the mosque is full of worshippers. The top of the minaret is where the **mu'adhin** traditionally stands.

The mu'adhin

Every mosque has a mu'adhin (sometimes spelled muezzin) whose job it is to call the people to prayer five times a day. The Call to Prayer is called the **adhan**. Some mu'adhins still chant the adhan from the minaret tower, but in many mosques in towns and cities there is now a loudspeaker system which means that the adhan can be heard more clearly. It also saves the mu'adhin the climb to the top of the tower!

The Call to Prayer

The adhan begins with the words 'Allahu-Akbar'. In English, it translates like this:

God is most great,
God is most great,
God is most great,
God is most great,
I bear witness that
there is no god but Allah,
I bear witness that
there is no god but Allah,
I bear witness that
Muhammad is a messenger of Allah,
I bear witness that
Muhammad is a messenger of Allah,
Come to prayer,
Come to prayer,
Come to security,
Come to security,
God is most great,
God is most great,
There is no god but Allah.

When the mu'adhin makes the Call for the first prayer of the day, he also includes the words 'Prayer is better than sleep!'

▶ *An American Muslim making the Call to Prayer.*

Inside a mosque

You can find the places mentioned in this book on the map on page 44.

Muslims take off their shoes before they enter a **mosque**, so that it is kept clean for prayer. In most mosques there are shoe racks outside the door, though in some large mosques people keep their shoes with them in a bag. This avoids having to find them among thousands of other pairs at the end of the service. After they have removed their shoes, they perform **wudu** – washing to make themselves fit for prayer.

Near the entrance of a mosque there may be a notice-board which can be used to let worshippers know about things that may interest them. There may also be a row of clocks which show the prayer times for that day. These will vary depending on the country and the season, because they take place according to the position of the sun.

There is no furniture in the main room of a mosque. This always makes it seem large and spacious. The floor is usually covered with carpets. Sometimes, there is a design on the carpet. Individual mats may be used, with designs of Makkah or a famous mosque. Both the patterned carpet and the mats are intended to help the worshippers make neat rows, and help them face in the right direction. No one has a particular place, because everyone is equal in front of **Allah**, so it does not matter whether they are at the back or the front.

▼ *The mihrab in the Mosque of the Prophet, Madinah.*

The mihrab

In every mosque there is an alcove or arch set into one wall, which shows the **qiblah**, the direction of Makkah. This is called the **mihrab**. It is often very beautifully decorated. It may have tiles, and texts from the **Qur'an** written into it. The prayer leader usually stands in front of the mihrab.

The minbar

At the front of the mosque, usually at the right-hand side of the mihrab, is the **minbar**. This is a raised platform where the **imam** stands when he gives the address at prayers. Some minbars are very decorated, others may be just a simple platform, or just a flight of stairs. The idea is to raise the imam so that everyone in the mosque can see and hear him clearly.

Decorations

There are never any pictures in a mosque. Muhammad said that they must not be used, because there was a danger that people might begin to worship them. (Muslims regard any pictures of Allah or holy beings as blasphemy, in other words insulting Allah.) Instead of pictures, the mosque is beautifully decorated. The carpets are often made in rich colours

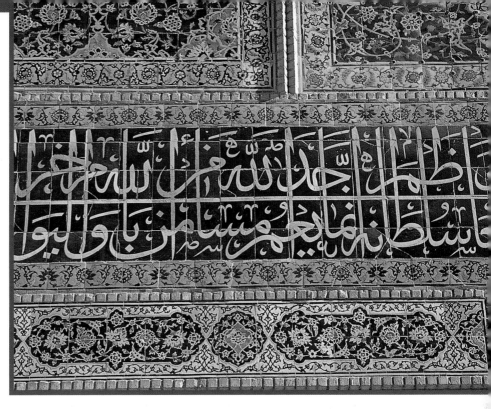

▲ *This calligraphy is part of the decoration in a mosque in Iran.*

with patterns on them. Green is popular because it was Muhammad's favourite colour, and a rich turquoise blue is often used, too. The walls may have tiles or other paintings to make them beautiful. These may be pictures of flowers or plants, or geometric patterns. Marble pillars and dangling glass chandeliers are other ways in which a mosque can be made to look special.

Calligraphy

A special form of decoration is Islamic **calligraphy**. Calligraphy is the art of beautiful handwriting, and especially the art of making writing into pictures. It began when people began to write out verses from the Qur'an. They wanted to make them as beautiful as possible, to show how much they valued them. At first, the words were written on paper or parchment, using sharpened reeds dipped in ink. Later, tiles and pottery began to be decorated in this way too. Pictures can be made using letters, phrases from the Qur'an, or prayers. In the mosque, these can help the people to worship.

Musa's view

Musa is 12, and lives with his family in London.

I go to the **madrasah** for **Islamiat** (the study of Islam) on Saturdays, and usually for a couple of hours after school, so that I can learn **Arabic** and the Qur'an. Sometimes if I've had a hard day at school, it feels like doing extra work, but it's totally different from the way we work at school. I know some of the Qur'an off by heart now, and the more I learn Arabic the easier it is to understand. The imam who teaches us really tries hard to make us understand, and I enjoy feeling that I'm learning more about something that's so important.

Major places of worship

The Ka'bah

The **Ka'bah** is the most important building in the world for Muslims. It is Islam's holiest shrine. It stands in the central courtyard of the Great Mosque, in the centre of Makkah. It was already very old when Muhammad was alive, and no one really knows where it came from. There are two traditions. One says that it was built by Adam, the first man, as the first place in the world to worship **Allah**. Then it was rebuilt by the **prophet** Ibrahim and his son Isma'il to thank Allah for saving Isma'il's life (see page 33). Ibrahim is the prophet whom Jews and Christians call Abraham. The other tradition says that it was built first by Ibraham and Isma'il. Both accounts agree that it was built to worship Allah.

You can find the places mentioned in this book on the map on page 44.

At the time of Muhammad, the Ka'bah was a centre of worship, but worship of **idols**. It contained over 360 statues and altars, for worshipping many different gods. Many people came to worship these idols. This was one of the reasons why Makkah was an important centre of **pilgrimage** and such a rich city at the time of Muhammad. After Muhammad had converted the Makkans to Islam, all the idols were thrown out of the city, and the Ka'bah became a centre of worship for Allah. Ever since, it has been the shrine that all Muslims face when they pray.

The Ka'bah is built of brick, and is cube-shaped (ka'bah means 'cube'). It measures 15 metres long by 10 metres wide and 14 metres high. Inside it is a room whose walls are covered with quotations from the **Qur'an**. It is a rare and special privilege for a Muslim to be allowed to pray inside the Ka'bah. He can pray and – for the only time in his life – face alternately in all four directions as he prays.

During the time of the **Hajj**, the Ka'bah is covered with a black cloth beautifully decorated with the words of the Qur'an in gold embroidery. At the end of Hajj the cloth is cut into small pieces and pilgrims are able to take these home with them.

▼ *The Black Stone.*

The Black Stone

In one corner of the Ka'bah is the Black Stone. This is an oval stone about 18 cm long which is probably a meteorite. Today it is set in silver. It was very old at the time of Muhammad and there are many stories about it. One story says that Adam found it in the desert, when it was gleaming white, but the sins of human beings have caused it to turn black. Another story says that angels took it to heaven for safe keeping at the time of the Great Flood, and returned it when Ibrahim and Isma'il rebuilt the Ka'bah.

The Mosque of the Prophet

The **Mosque** of the Prophet is in Madinah and was built over the place where Muhammad's body was buried. Muhammad's tomb lies beneath a green dome, and the mosque has been extended and enlarged several times since his death. The mosque also contains the graves of the **khalifahs** Abu Bakr and Umar. It is an important place of pilgrimage for Muslims, especially when they have been on Hajj to Makkah.

The Mosque of the Dome of the Rock

The Mosque of the Dome of the Rock is in Jerusalem. It was built in the seventh century CE and was restored in the sixteenth century. Jerusalem is the third holiest city for Muslims, after Makkah and Madinah. They believe that this mosque marks the place where Muhammad was taken to heaven on the Night of the Journey (see page 35). They also believe that the rock on which this mosque is built is the place where the call to judgement will be sounded on the **Day of Judgement**.

▲ *Inside the Mosque of the Dome of the Rock in Jerusalem.*

Muhammad and the Black Stone

When Muhammad was a young man, the Ka'bah was being repaired, and the Black Stone had been removed. When it was due to be replaced, a squabble broke out among the different tribes in Makkah as to who should be given the honour of carrying it. Muhammad settled the quarrel by spreading a rug on the ground, and lifting the Black Stone onto it. The heads of the tribes then took a corner of the rug each, so that they could all carry it. Muslims say that it was because of incidents like these that Muhammad was so respected, even before he began to have **revelations** from Allah.

27

Hajj – pilgrimage to Makkah

Every Muslim who is healthy and who can afford it is expected to go on a **pilgrimage** to Makkah at least once in their life. To be a true **Hajj**, the pilgrimage must take place between 8 and 13 Dhul-Hijjah, the last month of the Muslim year. Every year, about two million pilgrims go to Makkah at this time. Pilgrimage at other times of the year is called **Umrah**, and is not considered so important.

Pilgrims on Hajj wear special clothes called ihram.

Ihram

Whilst they are on Hajj, pilgrims are expected to live in a special way called **ihram**. They should not swear or quarrel. Any sexual contact is forbidden, even if husbands and wives are travelling together. To show that the thoughts of all pilgrims are pure, women do not cover their faces, even if they normally do so. No one wears jewellery or cosmetics, or uses scented soap. Pilgrims do not cut their hair or trim their nails.

The special clothes for Hajj are also called ihram. Every man wears two white sheets without seams, one wrapped around the lower body, the other draped over the left shoulder. They do not cover their heads, though they may carry an umbrella as protection against the sun. Women wear a plain dress with long sleeves, leaving only their face and hands uncovered. All pilgrims go barefoot or in open sandals. Everyone dresses in the same way, so that there are no barriers between rich and poor. Everyone is equal before **Allah**.

Performing Hajj

As soon as a pilgrim arrives in Makkah, they hurry to the **Ka'bah**, and circle it seven times. They walk quickly, running if possible. Those close enough touch or kiss the Black Stone. Those further away raise their hands towards it. Then they go to pray near Maqam Ibrahim (Ibrahim's place). They hurry seven times between two small hills not far from the Ka'bah. Today, the hills are linked by a broad corridor. This reminds pilgrims how Ibrahim's wife Hajar ran between the two hills desperately looking for water for her son Isma'il. The well they believe Hajar found is called the Well of Zamzam, in the courtyard of the Great **Mosque**. Pilgrims drink from it and often collect some water to take home for friends and family.

You can find the places mentioned in this book on the map on page 44.

Wuquf

On 9 Dhul-Hijjah, the pilgrims travel to the Plain of Arafat, about 20 km from Makkah. Here they take part in the 'stand before Allah', called **wuquf**. This is the most important part of the pilgrimage. They stand from midday to sunset, thinking about Allah, and asking him to forgive all the wrong things they have done in their life. Muslims believe that if it is properly performed, wuquf means that all a person's sins are forgiven. The pilgrims return to Muzdalifah for the evening prayers and to camp overnight.

On the morning of 10 Dhul-Hijjah, the pilgrims go to Mina, where there are three stone pillars. They throw stones at these, as a reminder of how Ibrahim drove away the devil who was tempting him. After the first pillar has been stoned, pilgrims **sacrifice** a sheep or a goat. This is part of the festival of Id-ul-Adha, in which Muslims all over the world take part. Male pilgrims then either cut their hair or shave their heads, and women cut off a lock of their hair. They do this because it is what Muhammad did. They take off their special pilgrim clothes and return to their normal clothes. They camp at Mina for three more days, and then travel back to Makkah for a last walk around the Ka'bah. They drink as much as they can from the Well of Zamzam, and then the Hajj is ended. Some pilgrims return home, others stay to visit other holy sites in the area.

▼ *The plain of Arafat during Hajj.*

Hussain's view

Hussain is 14 and lives in Lahore, Pakistan.

My uncle went on Hajj a couple of years ago. It's so popular now you have to apply for a place. The whole family helped him get ready, making sure he didn't forget anything. In a lot of families, I know people club together to get the money to send one person. We couldn't wait for him to come home and tell us all about it. I just can't imagine that many people all gathered together. He said that it's safer now than it used to be, but in the old days people sometimes used to be crushed to death in the crowd. He brought us a bottle of water from the Well of Zamzam. We looked at his ihram clothes, which he brought home so that when he dies he can be buried in them. He said the whole Hajj was a wonderful experience and not like anything else in the whole of his life. I really look forward to the day when I can go.

Celebrations – Ramadan

Ramadan is the ninth month of the Muslim calendar. Every year, for the 29 or 30 days of this month, Muslims **fast** during the hours of daylight. The instruction to perform the fast comes from the **Qur'an**, and the observance of it goes right back to the days of Muhammad.

All eating finishes before dawn, so the day starts well before this. To avoid confusion, lists are published in different places

▲ *Giving thanks before breaking the fast during Ramadan.*

announcing the time when fasting must begin and end. Breakfast is usually a high-energy meal, to give a good start to the day. At sunset, there is a light snack, followed by a main meal later.

Why do Muslims fast?

Muhammad taught his followers that the fasting is very important, because it is a sign that they have submitted to **Allah**. It shows that Allah is the most important thing in their life – far more important than food and drink. It is also a great 'leveller'. Hunger is the same for everyone, rich and poor, so it reminds them that everyone is equal in Allah's eyes.

Who fasts?

Eating and drinking nothing all day is very difficult, especially in hot countries. In Europe and America it is not so hot, but the days can be far longer. Muslims believe that Ramadan is intended to be hard but not cruel, so some groups of people are excused from fasting. The very old and the very young are not expected to fast at all. Children from about the age of seven will begin to fast, but they are not expected to fast for the whole month until they are about twelve. Anyone who is ill, or a woman who is pregnant, is not expected to fast. Anyone travelling is not expected to fast but should make up for missed days when they return home. If someone's health prevents them from fasting (for example, diabetes is an illness where fasting could be fatal) they are expected to pay a sum of money which would buy a meal for 60 people instead. If someone breaks the fast without a good reason, they should fast for an extra 60 days, to make up.

What happens if a Muslim does not fast?

There are no punishments if Muslims do not fast. Muslims believe that the judge of someone's behaviour is Allah, who knows and sees everything. At the end of the world, everyone will get what they deserve, according to how they have lived. To cheat on the fast is cheating yourself, and cheating Allah. Muhammad taught that there are two rewards for everyone who fasts. One is knowing that you have fasted successfully, with the joy of eating again afterwards. The other is the reward that you will be given by Allah on the **Day of Judgement**.

The Muslim calendar

Islam follows a lunar year. This means that each new month begins on the night of the new moon. A month therefore lasts 29 or 30 days, so is slightly shorter than the 'Western' calendar months. This means that each year is about ten days shorter than a Western year. The months move back through the seasons, year by year, so that over several years each month will have occurred in every season. This is particularly important for celebrations like Ramadan, which involve fasting during daylight hours. Away from the equator, days vary in length throughout the year, so the time of fasting is a great deal longer in July than in January.

How to live during Ramadan

Ramadan is called the holy month, and Muslims try to live especially pure lives during this month. Muslims who smoke try not to, and they do not have any sexual contacts during the day. They spend more time reading the Qur'an, and try to spend extra time on religious matters. Many Muslims try to read through the whole of the Qur'an during the month. During the last ten days of Ramadan, some Muslims go on a **retreat** to the **mosque**. They take only basic necessities with them, and live as simply as possible, reading the Qur'an and thinking about their religion. This was how Muhammad spent the last ten days of Ramadan. The festival of Id-ul-Fitr marks the end of Ramadan.

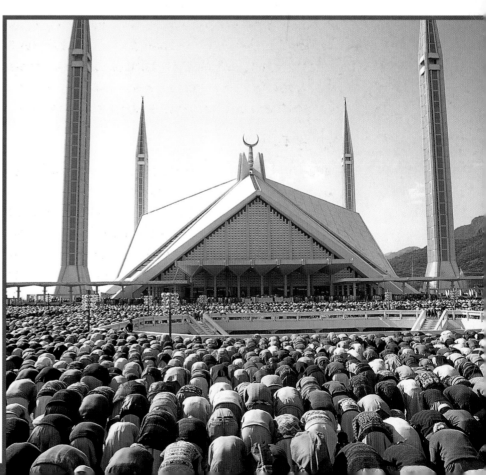

▶ *Prayers at a mosque in Pakistan during Ramadan.*

Celebrations – Id-ul-Fitr and Id-ul-Adha

Id-ul-Fitr

Id (sometimes spelled Eid) is the Muslim word for festival. Id-ul-Fitr is the festival that ends **Ramadan**, the month when Muslims **fast**. Before the festival begins, everyone gives money to charity. This is called Zakat-ul-Fitr. The idea is that everyone should have enough to be able to celebrate the festival properly.

On the night that Ramadan ends, many Muslims do not go to bed. They meet friends outside, and watch together for the new moon. When it appears, the new month of Shawwal has begun. The festival can begin!

In olden days, the beginning of the festival was announced by the **mu'adhin** calling the people to prayer from the **mosque**. Today, it is announced on radio and television. As soon as the festival has officially begun, everyone rushes to greet each other. They wish each other Happy Id ('Id mubarak'), and there is much handshaking and hugging. Everyone is in a holiday mood, congratulating each other on completing the fast. People usually break the fast with a light snack. The evening prayers follow, and then the main meal of the day.

▼ New clothes for Id help to make the festival special.

On Id day, everyone wears their best (or new) clothes. There are special services at the mosque or place where large numbers of Muslims can meet. These are often the largest congregations of the year, and thousands of people may gather together to celebrate the festival. The main meal is at lunchtime, and is the best the family can afford. Most people meet with friends or relatives, and spend the rest of the day visiting or being visited. Id is a chance for people who have not seen each other for a long time to meet and talk. There are parties, and people exchange presents and cards. In Muslim countries Id is a three-day holiday.

Id-ul-Adha

Id-ul-Adha takes place in the month of Dhul-Hijjah. It is the most important festival of the Muslim year. It forms part of the **Hajj**, but it is celebrated by all Muslims all over the world.

Id-ul-Adha means 'Festival of Sacrifice'. It is the time when Muslims remember the story in the **Qur'an** about how Ibrahim was asked to **sacrifice** his son, Isma'il, as a test of his submission. He did not have to kill Isma'il, because as he was about to make the sacrifice he was told to sacrifice a ram instead. However, the point of the story is that Ibrahim was ready to sacrifice even the son whom he loved more than anything else, because he believed it was what **Allah** wanted.

The most important part of Id-ul-Adha is sacrificing an animal – sheep, goat, cow or camel. It is the duty of a Muslim man to know how to kill an animal so that it does not suffer, and the meat from it is **halal**. (In Western countries, slaughtering an animal at home is against the law. It must be done in an abattoir by someone who is specially trained.) The meat from the animal is divided up, and one-third of it is always given to the poor. At the time of the Hajj, the Saudi Ministry of **Pilgrimage** organizes the disposal and freezing of the carcasses, because there are so many pilgrims the meat cannot all be eaten at once.

▲ At Id-ul-Adha, pilgrims on Hajj shave their heads.

Zakah

Giving to people who are poor or in need is part of a Muslim's duty. This is called **Zakah** (or Zakat when followed by another word). Zakah is the third pillar of Islam. Muslims are expected to give 2.5 per cent of income they have received and not spent on essentials during a year. Zakat-ul-Fitr is the donation to the poor at Id-ul-Fitr, and it amounts to the cost of providing a meal for the whole family. Zakah is not paid openly, so that rich people do not receive false admiration and poor people are not ashamed of receiving it. Giving Zakah reminds Muslims that everything they have comes from Allah, and should be used for good.

Celebrations – the minor festivals

You can find the places mentioned in this book on the map on page 44.

For Muslims, festivals are not only important occasions for worshipping **Allah**, but also for putting right things that are wrong with your life. They are chances to remember the rest of the Muslim family throughout the world, and make up for things you have done wrong or have forgotten to do. Id-ul-Adha and Id-ul-Fitr are the only two major festivals for Muslims, but there are other days during the year that are important.

The Day of the Hijrah (1 Muharram)

This is celebrated on 1 Muharram, the first month of the year, so it is the Muslim New Year's Day. It remembers the journey that Muhammad made when he travelled to Madinah. Muslims regard this event as very important, because it was the beginning of the success of Islam. Muharram was declared to be the first month of the year by **Khalifah** Umar.

Ashura (10 Muharram)

This day was a traditional day of **fasting** before the time of Muhammad. According to Muslim tradition, it is the day when Nuh (Noah) left the Ark, and when Allah saved Musa (Moses) from the **Pharaoh**. The day is particularly important for Shi'ah Muslims, who remember the martyrdom of Husain (see page 13).

Mawlid an-Nabi (12 Rabi al-Awwal)

This is Muhammad's birthday, which probably fell on 20 August 570 CE. In many parts of the world, the day is celebrated with processions and meetings or lectures where events in Muhammad's life can be remembered. In some places there are 'birthday parties' for poor or under-privileged children. Some Muslims do not approve of giving so much importance to any human being, even Muhammad, and so do not approve of the celebrations.

◀ *In this mosque in the Yemen, the stained glass windows add to the beauty of the building.*

Laylat-ul-Mi'raj (27 Rajab)

This is the Night of the Journey. Muslims believe that on this night Muhammad made a miraculous journey with the angel Jibril from Makkah to Jerusalem. They rode on the back of an animal called al-Buraq (the Lightning) which was like a horse with wings. From Jerusalem, he was taken to heaven where he met and prayed with all the **prophets**, and was taught by Allah. Muslims believe that this was when Allah taught the importance of prayer five times a day. Some Muslims believe that this was a **vision** rather than that Muhammad was physically transported there. The **mosque** called the Dome of the Rock is built on the site where Muslims believe this happened.

Laylat-ul-Bara'at (14 Shabaan)

This is the night of the full moon before **Ramadan**. It is sometimes called the Gateway to Ramadan. For many Muslims it is a night to spend extra time reading the **Qur'an** and remembering that Muhammad began his preparations for Ramadan on this night.

Laylat-ul-Qadr (27 Ramadan)

This is the Night of Power, when Muslims remember Muhammad receiving his first **revelation** of the Qur'an. No one knows exactly when this happened, but it is usually celebrated on the 27th day of Ramadan. Many Muslims spend all night reading the Qur'an and thinking about its importance in their lives. In some places, it is traditional for groups of friends to meet and go to pray in several different mosques during the night.

▲ *A sixteenth-century illustration, from Iran, showing Muhammad's Night Journey. Notice that the Prophet's face is veiled, because to portray it would be blasphemous (insulting to Allah).*

The revelation on the Night of Power

Muslims believe that the Qur'an itself refers to the night when Muhammad was given the first revelation:

By the star when it sets! Your fellow man (Muhammad) is not making a mistake. He has not been misled. He is not speaking from mere impulse. The Qur'an is nothing less than that which was revealed to him. One mighty in power showed it to him, one full of wisdom.
(Surah 53: 1–10)

Family occasions – childhood

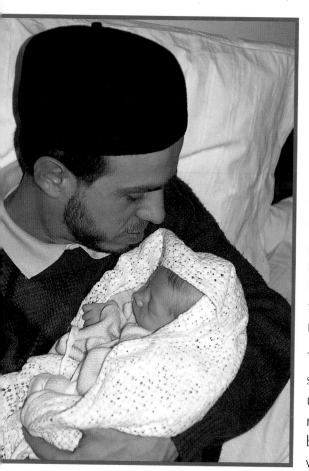

Islam teaches that babies are a gift from God. Having a large number of children is regarded as a great blessing. Muslims regard it as a duty of parents to bring their children up to become good Muslims.

When a baby is born, it is washed, and dressed or wrapped in a shawl. Then the baby is given to the head of the family, who whispers the **adhan** – the Call to Prayer – into its right ear. Then the Command to Worship – the command normally given when the congregation is ready to pray – is said softly into the left ear. Muslims believe that this has two purposes. It welcomes the baby into the family of Islam as soon as it is born, and it means that the first word the baby hears is '**Allah**'.

There is a custom of rubbing a tiny piece of sugar or honey on the baby's tongue. This is usually done by the oldest or most respected relative. It is a symbol of the hope that the baby's life will be sweet – that is, that the baby will grow up to be obedient and kind.

▲ *Whispering the adhan into a newborn baby's ear.*

Aqiqah

The ceremony called **aqiqah** is held when the baby is seven days old. Friends and relatives come to a feast, and the baby is given its name. Choosing the name for a baby is seen as one of the important duties of parents. Sometimes a traditional family name is used, sometimes the name of Muhammad or one of his family. A common choice for boys is one of the 99 names of God, with 'Abd' in front of it. Abd means 'servant of' in **Arabic**. This is a way of saying that the boy will be Allah's servant all through his life. Names suggesting that the child will be a servant of anything other than Allah are forbidden. It is quite common for the parents to stop using their own name when they have a child, and become known as the parents of the child. So for example, if the child is called Muhammad, the parents would become Abu Muhammad (father of Muhammad) and Umm Muhammad (mother of Muhammad).

At the aqiqah, the baby's head is shaved. The hair that is cut off is weighed and the value of an equal weight in silver is given to the poor. Even if the baby has been born with very little or no hair, a donation is still given. It often exceeds what the hair actually weighs.

Khitan

If the baby is a boy, he must be circumcised. This means cutting off the foreskin, the flap of skin which covers the end of the penis. **Khitan** is the Arabic word for circumcision. This may be done at the same time as the aqiqah or, if there is some reason to delay, it can be left until the boy is a few months old. Not to have a baby boy circumcised would be considered very neglectful by the parents.

Bismillah

Around the time that a child is four, some Muslims, particularly in India, have a ceremony called **Bismillah**. Bismillah means 'In the name of Allah', and the ceremony involves the child learning the words that begin all but one of the surahs in the **Qur'an**: 'In the name of Allah, the gracious, the merciful.'

The child learns how to say each word of the Arabic correctly, and is also taught how to pray. Whether or not they have been through a special ceremony, all Muslim children from about the age of four are expected to attend the **madrasah** at the **mosque**, to learn Arabic and learn about Islam.

The names of Allah

The Qur'an gives 99 names for Allah. Muslims use these names when they pray. Many Muslims have a string of 33 or 99 beads which they use when they pray, to allow them to remember Allah 99 times. Other Muslims use the finger joints of their right hand in the same way.

Some of the names are: the merciful, the compassionate, the forgiver, the generous, the affectionate, the kind, the gracious, the protector, the eternal, the creator, the holy one, the mighty, the wise one, the source of peace, guardian of faith and preserver of sanity.

▼ *Children attend the madrasah to learn more about Islam.*

Family occasions – marriage

In Muslim families, marriage is very important. Few Muslims stay single all their lives. Sexual relationships outside of marriage are forbidden. Marriage is important because it joins two families. For many young Muslim couples marriages are arranged by their parents. This means that older relatives suggest someone who they feel would be a suitable partner. In Muslim law, and in the **Hadith**, the young person has the right to disagree with the parents' choice. The law forbids forced marriages.

Muslims believe that the best relationships are based on suitability and knowing a person's background. If two people are compatible and suitable for each other, love can follow their marriage. In Western countries this has caused tension and problems in some families. Where Muslim boys and girls grow up seeing friends choosing to go out with people of the opposite sex, they sometimes feel that they want to do the same. Other Muslims are happy for their parents to choose their partner, feeling that they will make a good choice.

▲ *A Western Muslim wedding group.*

Marrying more than one person

At the time of Muhammad, a man could marry as many women as he wanted. The **Qur'an** changed this, saying that a man should marry no more than four women. Even then, the condition is that all the wives must be treated exactly the same and if he thinks he cannot do this he should marry only one. Today, this is generally accepted to be impossible, so most men only marry once. However, some men do marry a second woman, usually if the first one becomes ill or is unable to have children. In Western countries, it is illegal to marry more than one person at a time.

Other religions

According to Islamic teaching, a child takes the religion of their father. For this reason, a Muslim woman may only marry a Muslim man, but a Muslim man may marry a Christian or Jewish woman. These three religions have teachings in common. If a Muslim man wishes to marry a member of any other religion, he can only do so if the woman converts to Islam.

The marriage

A Muslim wedding is a simple occasion. There are readings from the Qur'an, an exchange of vows in front of witnesses, and prayers. The **imam** may be present, but this is not required. Both partners must sign the **nikah** (wedding contract). This can include anything that they both want to make a condition of the marriage. It cannot include anything that would go against the purpose of marriage – so, for example, it could not include an agreement that they will not live together.

The signing of the nikah may take place months or even years before the couple begin to live together. The wedding party or **walimah** takes place within three days of them beginning to live together. It usually consists of a meal for friends and relatives. They give presents, usually money. In some countries, the walimah is a huge, expensive party which lasts for days. Muhammad disapproved of this, especially where it causes serious financial hardship for the families.

Divorce

Muhammad described divorce as 'the most detestable act that God has permitted'. Muslims regard divorce as a last resort. However, it teaches that if the marriage has truly failed, there is no point in the couple staying together. Once the divorce is final, an ex-husband has no further responsibility for his wife. Either person is free to marry again after divorce.

▲ A Muslim bride wearing traditional dress.

Salman's view

Salman is 15 and lives in Melbourne, Australia.

My sister Aisha got married last year. Her husband Rashid is the son of friends of my parents, so we'd known him for a long time. The marriage was sort of half arranged, because my father and Rashid's father had thought about it a long time ago, but then when Father asked Aisha, she suggested marrying Rashid. They got married in the mosque and there were loads of people there. All the women had spent ages getting food ready for the party afterwards and we had a really good time.

Family occasions – death and beyond

When a Muslim is known to be about to die, friends and relatives are sent for, and gather around the bed. The person asks their forgiveness for anything they may have done wrong. They ask forgiveness from God, too. If possible, the last words the dying person says are the **Shahadah**: 'There is no God except **Allah**, and Muhammad is the messenger of Allah.'

As soon as possible after death, the body is washed. Muslims prefer that this is done by relatives. Then it may be anointed with spices and wrapped in a shroud of white cloth. This may be the **ihram** cloth from the person's **Hajj**. Someone who has died a **martyr** is buried unwashed, in the clothes in which they were killed, preferably at the place where they died.

Funerals should be as simple as possible. No extravagance is allowed, because death happens to everyone, and it does not matter then if they were rich or poor. Muslims prefer that a body should be carried to the burial ground rather than being placed in a vehicle. It should be placed in a grave in contact with the earth. Coffins should not be used unless there is some reason for them. Muslims prefer a body to be buried with the face turned to the right, facing Makkah. For this reason, they prefer their own burial plots, because those designed for other religions may not allow Muslim graves to be placed in the right direction. Simple headstones may record the name of someone who has died, but Muslims do not believe that it is right for large sums of money to be spent on very ornate memorials.

▲ *A funeral at Regent's Park Mosque, London.*

After death

Muslims believe that when someone dies, their soul waits for the **Day of Judgement**. This period of waiting is known as being 'in **barzakh**'. The Day of Judgement may not happen for hundreds or even thousands of years, but time in barzakh is not the same as time on Earth, and it will pass in a flash. Then the Day of Judgement – the end of the world – will happen.

▲ *A Muslim graveyard in Pakistan.*

For Muslims, this life on Earth is the shorter part of each human being's existence. It is a test that decides what happens in the next part, after death. If someone has persisted in evil ways and refused to acknowledge that they are wrong and ask Allah's forgiveness while they were still alive, it will be too late. There will be no forgiveness at the end of time.

Muslims teach that after the Day of Judgement will come **akhirah** – life after death. Those who have gained Allah's forgiveness will go to **Paradise**, which is described as a garden of happiness. This will be a state of joy and peace. People who have not believed will go to Hell, a place of burning and torment. Muslims accept that the afterlife is such a totally different dimension that we have no words to describe it.

Angels

Muslims believe that angels are messengers of Allah. They believe that they are creatures of light who are in touch with human beings all the time. When someone prays or thinks about God, the angels gather round and join in. Human beings only see angels on very rare occasions, but this does not mean that they are not there. They can take any form they wish. For example, when Muhammad first saw the angel Jibril it was as an enormous creature who covered the horizon and had thousands of wings. When Jibril appeared to Maryam (Mary) to announce the birth of Isa (Jesus) it was as a human being.

Muslims believe that every person has two special angels with them all the time. They keep a record of all good and bad things the person does throughout their life. At the Day of Judgement this will be given to the person, who will be able to work out for themselves what their destiny should be. At the end of formal prayers, Muslims turn their heads from side to side to greet these angels.

What does it mean to be a Muslim?

In the community

Muslims are very conscious of the worldwide family of Muslims, called the **Ummah**. The fact that someone is a Muslim is far more important than which country they come from or what colour their skin is. This has always been true, but it is probably becoming more so as increasing numbers of Muslims come from non-Arab nations. Although many people, especially in the West, tend to associate Islam with Arabs, at the beginning of the twenty-first century, only one-sixth of all Muslims are Arab.

Islam encourages people to be sociable, and meeting friends is very important. Muhammad recommended that you should not go for more than three days without visiting a friend! Guests should be invited to meals wherever possible, and inviting only wealthy people is not approved of. This means that there is always the opportunity to give to the poor. Muhammad once said, 'An ignorant person who is generous is nearer to **Allah** than a person full of prayer who is miserly.' Islam teaches that any giving should be done discreetly.

Islam teaches that both men and women should dress modestly. For men, this means being covered from the waist to the knees. For women, it means that head, arms and legs should be covered. Muslims believe that wearing short, tight or see-through clothing which is intended to show off the body is wrong. They feel that it tempts men, which is neither kind nor fair, and is degrading to women. When they are outside the home, many Muslim women dress so that as little as possible of their body can be seen. This includes wearing a full-length dress and a veil or scarf over their head. This is called **hijab**.

◀ Family life is very important to Muslims.

At work

Islam teaches that work is necessary and important. Provided that the job does not conflict with any of the teachings of Islam, what is important is that it is done carefully and well. Traditionally it is the woman's job to look after the home and the family. The man's job is to provide the means for the woman to be able to do this. Islam teaches that a mother is a priceless treasure, and many women feel that creating a loving home and family is the most important job they could ever do.

In the home

Respect for other people is an important teaching of Islam. Respect for older people is especially important. They have had more experience of life and so they are wiser and their opinions should be listened to. Parents should be cared for in their old age, because they cared for their children when the children were too young to look after themselves. The concept of special homes where old people can be 'put away' is one that many Muslims find difficult to understand.

▲ For many Muslim women, creating a loving home and family is the most valuable job they could have.

Shari'ah

Shari'ah means 'the path'. It is the code of behaviour for Muslims. According to Muslim teaching, actions are divided into five groups. There are actions that must be done (e.g. **fasting** during Ramadan), actions that are recommended (e.g. forgiving other people wrongs they have done), actions that are up to a person's conscience, actions that are disapproved of but not forbidden (e.g. divorce) and actions that are strictly forbidden (e.g. worshipping other gods). Actions in the individual conscience group include most things in everyday life, and a person should decide for themselves what to do, in the light of the teachings of the **Qur'an** and of Muhammad. Then they, like all Muslims, will be able to say, 'To Allah we belong and to Him we return' (surah 2: 156).

Map

The globe on the right shows the location of the map below.

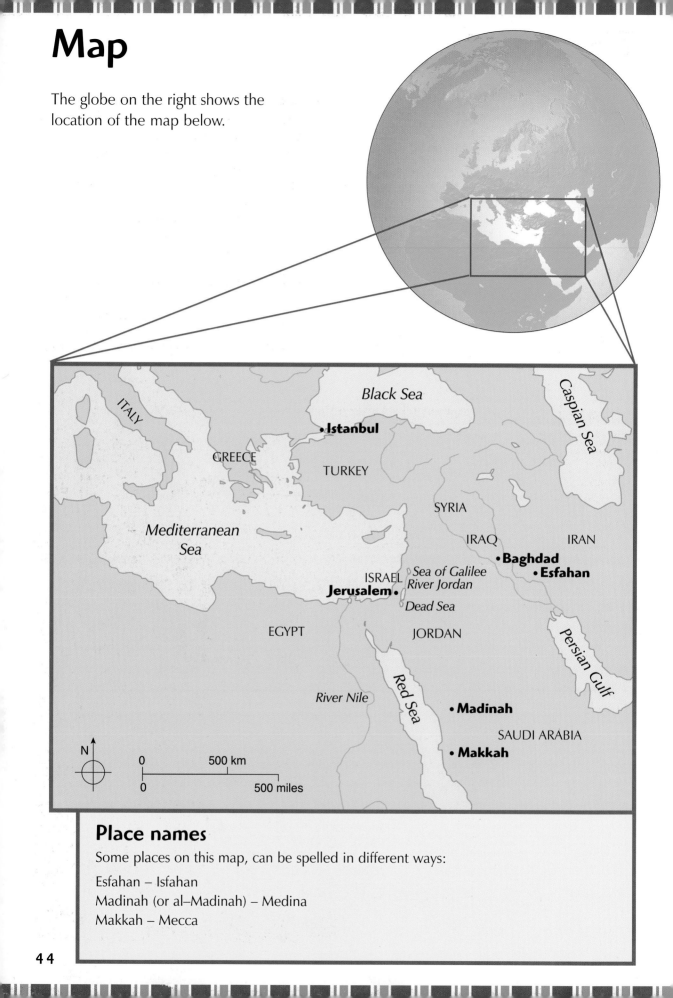

Place names

Some places on this map, can be spelled in different ways:

Esfahan – Isfahan
Madinah (or al–Madinah) – Medina
Makkah – Mecca

Timechart

Major events in World history

BCE **3000–1700** Indus valley civilization flourished

2500 Pyramids in Egypt built

1800 Stonehenge completed

1220 Ramses II builds the Temple of Amon (Egypt)

1000 Nubian Empire (countries around the Nile) begins & lasts until c350 CE

776 First Olympic games

450s Greece is a centre of art and literature under Pericles

BCE **336–323** Conquests of Alexander the Great

300 Mayan civilization begins

200 Great Wall of China begun

48 Julius Caesar becomes Roman Emperor

CE **79** Eruption of Vesuvius destroys Pompeii

161–80 Golden Age of the Roman Empire under Marcus Aurelius

330 Byzantine Empire begins

868 First printed book (China)

c1000 Leif Ericson may have discovered America

1066 Battle of Hastings, Norman conquest of Britain

1300 Ottoman Empire begins (lasts until 1922)

1325 Aztec Empire begins (lasts until 1521)

1400 Black Death kills one person in three throughout China, North Africa and Europe

1452 Leonardo da Vinci born

1492 Christopher Columbus sails to America

1564 William Shakespeare born

1620 Pilgrim Fathers arrive in what is now Massachusetts, USA

1648 Taj Mahal built

1768–71 Captain Cook sails to Australia

1776 American Declaration of Independence

1859 Charles Darwin publishes *Origin of Species*

1908 Henry Ford produces the first Model T Ford car

1914–18 World War I

1929 Wall Street Crash and the Great Depression

1939–45 World War II

1946 First computer invented

1953 Chemical structure of DNA discovered

1969 First moon landings

1981 AIDS virus diagnosed

1984 Scientists discover a hole in the ozone layer

1989 Berlin Wall is torn down

1991 Break-up of the former Soviet Union

1994 Nelson Mandela becomes President of South Africa

1997 An adult mammal, Dolly the sheep, is cloned for the first time

2000 Millennium celebrations take place all over the world

Major events in Islamic history

CE **570** birth of Muhammad

595 Muhammad marries Khadijah

610 Muhammad receives first revelation from the angel Jibril

622 The Hijrah ('migration') – Muhammad's journey to Madinah

624 Battle at Badr between Muhammad's followers and people of Makkah

625 Battle at Uhud

628 Treaty made with Makkans

630 Muhammad claims Makkah for Islam

632 Muhammad dies

637 Muslims gain control of Jerusalem

642 Muslims control Egypt

644–656 Khadifah Uthman ensures that the complete Qur'an is written down

680 Husain killed (remembered by Shi'as at the Ashura festival)

690s Dome of the Rock mosque completed

711 Muslims conquer Spain

762–766 Baghdad built (at that time the largest city on earth)

c850–932 Al-Razi (Muslim doctor and scholar)

878 Disappearance of the Mahdi (the Hidden Imam)

1025 Mahmud of Ghazni gains power in many Indian cities

1050–1122 Umar Khayyam (astronomer and Sufi poet)

1058–1111 Al-Ghazzali (one of the greatest Muslim scholars)

1138–1193 Salah ud Din Yusuf (Saladin) – great Muslim soldier and leader

1207–73 Jalal ud-Din Rumi (great Turkish Sufi mystic called the Mawlana)

1332–1406 Ibn Khaldun (great Muslim historian)

1489–1588 Sinan, Muslim architect (credited with building over 3000 mosques)

1520–1566 Suleiman the Magnificent (great Muslim leader)

1550 Sinan builds Suleimaniye Mosque, Istanbul (considered his finest)

1571–1629 Abbas I of Iran (established Isfahan as the capital of Iran)

1609 Blue Mosque in Istanbul begun

1857 British capture of Delhi ends 1000 years of Muslim rule in India

1947 Pakistan created as a Muslim country in the Indian sub-continent

1953 Enlargement of the Prophet's Mosque in Madinah

1979 Establishment of the Islamic Republic of Iran.

Glossary

adhan	the Call to Prayer
akhirah	life after death
Allah	Arabic name for God
aqiqah	child-naming ceremony
Arabic	language of Muslim worship and national language in parts of the Middle East and North Africa
Ayatollah	leader of Shi'ah Muslims
barzakh	period between death and the Day of Judgement
Bismillah	first words of the Qur'an (also a ceremony for children in some Muslim countries)
calligraphy	art of beautiful writing
Day of Judgement	end of the world, when Allah will judge everyone
du'a	personal prayers
eternal	lasting for ever
fast	go without food and drink for religious reasons
Hadith	teachings of Muhammad
hafiz	title given to someone who has learned the Qur'an off by heart
Hajj	pilgrimage to Makkah
halal	permitted (food that Muslims can eat)
haram	forbidden (food that Muslims cannot eat)
hijab	'veil' – used to describe the modest dress worn by Muslim women
hijrah	'departure' or 'emigration' – Muhammad's journey to Madinah
idols	statue worshipped as a god
ihram	special way of living for Hajj, and special clothes that are worn
imam	Muslim leader and teacher
Islamiat	study of Islam at the madrasah
jihad	struggle against evil to live in the way that Allah wants
Ka'bah	most important Muslim shrine in Makkah
khalifah	early leader of Islam
khitan	circumcision (removing the foreskin from the penis)
kursi	special stool used to rest the Qur'an on
madrasah	school at the mosque
martyr	someone who dies for what they believe

masjid	Arabic name for a mosque
meditate	to think deeply, especially about spiritual matters
mihrab	arch that shows the direction of Makkah
minaret	tower of a mosque
minbar	platform in a mosque used for preaching
mosque	Muslim place of worship
mu'adhin	man who calls Muslims to prayer
nikah	marriage contract
niyyah	intention (the motive which lies behind an action)
Paradise	garden of happiness for life with Allah after death
Pharaoh	Egyptian king
pilgrimage	journey for religious reasons
prophet	messenger from God
prostrate	bow down, to show submission
qiblah	direction of Makkah
Qur'an	Muslim holy book
rak'ah	set of positions for Muslim prayers
Ramadan	ninth month of the Muslim calendar when Muslims fast during daylight hours
retreat	special time of prayer and meditation
revelations	spiritual experiences in which something is revealed (e.g. Muhammad receiving the Qur'an)
sacrifice	killing something so that its life can be an offering
Salah	prayer
Sawm	fasting
Shahadah	the Declaration of Faith
shrine	holy place
Ummah	the worldwide Muslim family
Umrah	'lesser pilgrimage'
vision	dream-like religious experience
walimah	wedding party
wudu	special washing before prayer
wuquf	'stand before Allah' (while on Hajj)
Zakah	giving to charity

Index